16th October 2021

Dear Chris,

I saw this book in Grantown-on-Spey over the summer, and was thinking of you and our salmon ladder visit in Pitlochry I think!

Lots of love,
Ant x.

A SPEYSIDE ODYSSEY

A Natural History
of the Atlantic Salmon

Norman Matheson

Matador
9 Priory Business Park,
Wistow Road, Kibworth Beauchamp,
Leicestershire. LE8 0RX
Tel: 0116 279 2299
Email: books@troubador.co.uk
Web: www.troubador.co.uk/matador
Twitter: @matadorbooks

ISBN 978 1838591 182

British Library Cataloguing in Publication Data.
A catalogue record for this book is available from the British Library.

Printed by CPI Group (UK) Ltd, Croydon, CR0 4YY
Typeset in 12pt Sabon by Troubador Publishing Ltd, Leicester, UK

Matador is an imprint of Troubador Publishing Ltd

For the pools of Spey and A'en
For their distant hills
For their wildlife and
For the wild flowers
That bloom along their banks.

Contents

HRH THE PRINCE CHARLES, DUKE OF ROTHESAY

"A Speyside Odyssey" is an evocative celebration of natural history set in the captivatingly beautiful area of Northeast Scotland.

It gives me enormous pleasure to commend the work of Norman Matheson, whose unrivalled knowledge and infectious passion for the fascinating story of Atlantic salmon is greatly enhanced by his own splendid watercolour illustrations.

Today, more than ever, with the challenges of falling salmon stocks in many of our Scottish rivers, we require a better understanding of the lifespan and journey of this most resourceful and determined of creatures.

It is a story that has long been an inspiration to me and I have no doubt that the charm and detail of Dr. Matheson's book will provide a memorable illustration of the salmon's life cycle against the backdrop of the natural beauty of Speyside.

The salmon that breed and return to our native Scottish rivers deserve our most strenuous efforts to provide them with a safer and more sustainable existence in the years to come.

It is all the more worthwhile when one remembers that Dr. Matheson has donated the proceeds of this publication to the work of the Atlantic Salmon Trust, a charity of which I am proud to be Patron. The Trust was formed in 1967 and is the U.K.'s only charity whose work is devoted exclusively to the conservation of wild Atlantic salmon and sea trout. The Trust's focus is on the whole lives of these fish, in both freshwater and marine environments. Their current priority is to find out why and where salmon and sea trout are dying through a major Acoustic Tracking project centred around the Moray Firth.

In offering my sincere congratulations to all involved in this publication, I know I express the hopes of so many that the future of Atlantic salmon will be preserved so that coming generations can share in this amazing story.

Sketch Map of
Northern Scotland

O INVERNESS

R. SPEY

R. LIVET

ABERDEEN O

R A'EN (AVON)

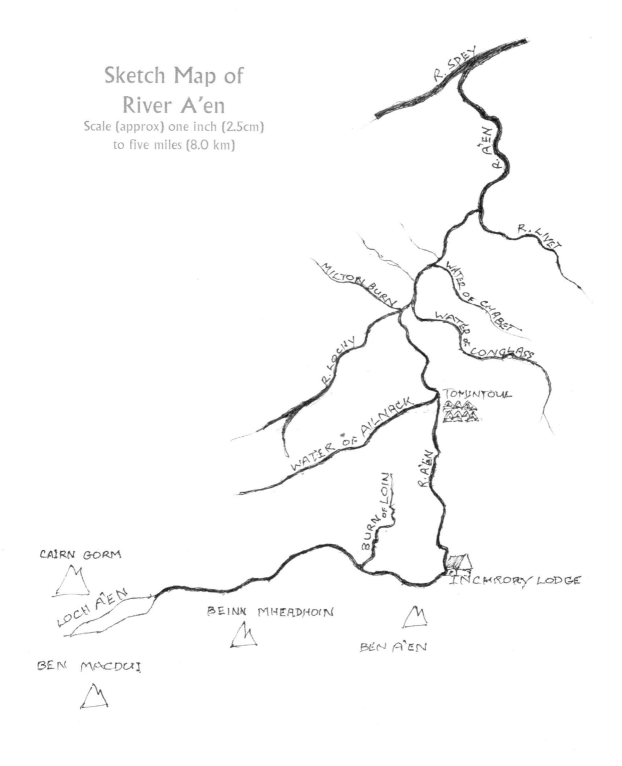

Sketch Map of
River A'en

Scale (approx) one inch (2.5cm)
to five miles (8.0 km)

Introduction

In the stillness of the distant hills the silence was broken only by the murmur of the burn that ran in the low ground, gurgling over rocks and spilling over beds of rough gravel. In winter months, the colour of the gravel was surprisingly variable. Much paler areas were in obvious contrast with the predominantly dark algal-stained surface. These lighter areas were characteristic of salmon redds where a hen fish had, by vigorous action of her tail fin, dug a trench for the deposition of several thousand eggs. After fertilisation by a shadowing mate, or occasionally by sexually precocious juvenile fish with sneaky intent, she would have covered the fertilised eggs with a deep layer of the excavated gravel. Salmon spawn is choice food for several predators, including salmon parr, trout and saw-bill ducks, and concealment is essential for its survival. In these redds, as in countless others in Scotland's rivers and burns, the remarkable life of a cohort of salmon began.

Rivers

The burn coursing through the remote glen was the Burn of Loin, that flows from the north through the vast Inchrory Estate to merge with the gin-clear water of A'en (Avon) a few miles upstream of Inchrory Lodge. Their confluence, in the shadow of the multiple rocky summits of Ben A'en, forms the Loin Pool, a small salmon holding pool replete with personal memories. A'en had already covered many miles from its origin in Loch A'en, clasped low in the mountainous embrace of Cairngorm, Ben Macdui and Beinn Mheadhoin, to become a small productive salmon river. Some nine miles (14km) downstream of Inchrory Lodge, it is joined by the Water of Ailnack, emerging from a precipitous defile on the Delnabo Estate near the village of Tomintoul. Tomintoul may now be more sober and sedate than in the past when it was deplored by the unco-guid as Sodom and Gomorrah, an epithet nowadays recalled with amusement.

Inchrory Lodge

As it flows onward through the secluded glen, known locally as A'enside (Avonside), the river continues to gain volume. Several burns draining the eastern slopes of the Cromdale Hills, together with the small River Lochy, join it on the left bank and two larger burns, Conglass and Chabet, on the right. Finally, flowing through the Ballindalloch Estate, it is joined by its main tributary, the River Livet, which drains the secluded basin of the fascinating Braes of Glenlivet as well as the farmland of the lower glen. Continuing through Ballindalloch land, A'en ends its long picturesque course by joining the majestic Spey, forming at their confluence the famous Junction Pool, well known to salmon anglers.

Junction Pool, Spey

Fast flowing Spey continues on a north-easterly course, through Speyside, renowned world-wide as the home of legendary malt whiskies. Several famous distilleries, the names of which are held in esteem by malt whisky connoisseurs, are within sight of the river. Spey is also one of the finest Scottish salmon rivers, the variable geography of which dictates the attraction of several prime angling beats. Downstream of the villages of Aberlour and Craigellachie, the arresting character of the river determines its two most attractive and prolific beats, Arndilly and Delfur, names that are the stuff of salmon fishermen's dreams. Downstream of Delfur, through the pools of Orton and the several beats on the Gordon Castle Estate, Spey finally forges a passage through extensive shingle banks, which during flood conditions are unstable. The river, as it enters the North Sea near the village of Spey Bay on the southern shore of the Moray Firth, is therefore subject to flood determined changes in its final course.

The Advent of Spring

In the early spring lapwings return to A'enside from lowland coastal flats. On disturbance, they rise from nesting sites in stubble fields, tumbling into the sky in round-winged lolloping flight, their distinctive cries filling the air. Although "peewit", another common name, roughly mimics their call, a wheezy "peez-y-weet" rising to a high-pitched final note is closer to it. Their nests, no more than simple depressions in the ground, commonly hold four beautiful tapered eggs, rich olive in colour, blotched in brown and black, nestling together, pointing towards the centre. Once the disturbance that sent them aloft abates, the lapwings spiral down to stand watchful with crests prominent and plumage glinting green and bronze in the watery sunshine of late March. Lapwings in characteristic flight display, filling the air with their evocative calls in the dormant fields of Strathavon, mark the unfolding drama of spring in a distinctive way.

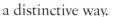
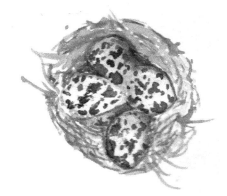

As the lapwings proclaim the early weeks of spring, the salmon eggs in the redds of Loin appear unchanged except that the tiny black eyes of the developing fish are now visible through translucent egg capsules. At a microscopic level, however, cell division and differentiation is advanced and, in a few more weeks, the creation of an infant fish will be complete.

The distant leafless birches will soon take on the lustrous purple sheen of buds poised to open and, in the woodland, one of nature's creative masterpieces emerges. Dispersed throughout the birch woods, emerging from the clasp of rich green crinkled leaves, is the beautiful common primrose (*Primula vulgaris*). The primrose, a bloom of the purest yellow, is the embodiment of simple perfection. Flowering unseen in secluded glades, it is the epitome of modesty. And its delicate perfume is captivating.

As the primroses fade, wood anemones (*Anemone nemorosa*) begin to flower, though much more sparsely, among the birches. Almost translucent white, or predominantly pink, nodding on single stems, opening to the sun, their charm is delicate and understated.

The Salmon Eggs Hatch

By the time the anemones are in bloom, the salmon eggs, having reached maturity, will begin to hatch with the emergence of tiny elongated fish-like forms (alevins). The alevins continue developing in the gravel of the redds for several more weeks, nourished by the resources of the egg, the yolk sac of which remains temporarily attached to the surface of the young fish. Finally, as the reserves of the yolk sac are exhausted, the alevins emerge from the gravel to face the unrelenting challenge of independent life as tiny salmon fry. Those that survive become distinctive as salmon parr. However, the population of surviving parr in any particular length of stream represents but a small fraction of the thousands of eggs deposited in the relevant redds.

Oystercatchers Return

As the immature fish continue their development into fry and parr, oystercatchers, flaunting their vivid orange beaks, announce their arrival from winter coastal habitats with loud incessant piping. Their high-pitched calling is a joyful harbinger of lengthening days and at night the shrill noise of their frequent nocturnal activity is remarkably soothing to one lying reflective in bed.

The Life of Salmon Parr

In early summer, as the small salmon parr metaphorically gird their loins against the harsh environment of their highland habitat, the wood anemones have faded and, in more open areas amongst the birches, sparse colonies of chickweed wintergreen (*Trientalis europaea*) come into bloom. For a wild flower of such exquisite beauty, pure white but crisper and more assertive than the wood anemone, its common name, chickweed wintergreen, is a decidedly inappropriate mouthful. The alternative name, arctic starflower, although more in tune with its elegance, is seldom heard. In recognition of its gem-like quality, chickweed wintergreen was chosen as the provincial flower of the Varmland province in Sweden.

As summer advances, parr become established in their chosen territories, taking up nutritional stations in shallow areas where flow and eddies determined by the contours of the stream bed help to minimise physical effort in maintaining position. During the next two or three years, as the tiny salmon parr become larger they venture into deeper and faster water, foraging for adequate nutrition to gain sufficient length, weight and strength for their arduous journey to the sea. In these infantile years they have to contend with ever-present predacious brown trout as well as many avian predators including herons, gulls, cormorants, goosanders and mergansers. Clearly, avoidance of such hazards may not be attributed to cognition but parr do react to unnatural movement such as the silhouette or shadow of man falling across their lies. In scattering for concealment they show innate protective reactions but they remain particularly vulnerable to the stealthy approach of brown trout and to the motionless heron poised in the shallows for the unwary to stray within striking distance of its lethal beak. Inevitably, many parr do not survive to complete the next stage of their life cycle, the transformation to smolts.

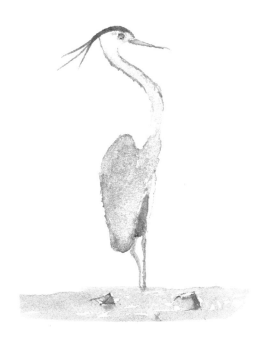

Transformation to Smolts

The stimuli that govern the changes that occur, at two or three years of age, whereby parr become smolts and set off towards the sea, are unknown. The most obvious change, transformation to a bright silvery appearance, attributed to the pigment guanin, evidently protects against the osmotic challenge of transposition from fresh water to a salt-water environment of considerably higher osmotic pressure. Surviving parr, two or three years old, will be influenced to leave the Loin Burn mainly in the late spring although a minority may leave in the previous autumn, taking months over the same journey. In addition, together with progeny from other spawning sites, parr forsake their habitual solitary mien to form small schools in which they swim downstream in the turbulent water of A'en and then by Spey to the sea. As the crow of the cliché flies, the distance from the Loin Burn to Spey Bay is roughly 100km, a figure irrelevant for juvenile salmon, which clearly face a much more tortuous and considerably longer journey, albeit assisted by the direction of flow. Smolt migration takes place mainly under the cover of darkness and incurs significant loss of life. Recent studies on the Aberdeenshire Dee have shown much higher losses during the fresh water phase of smolt life than has hitherto been appreciated, the presumption being that this is largely attributable to avian predation. However, each year some several hundred thousand smolts are expected to have successfully reached the estuary of Spey by the end of June.

Migration to the Feeding Grounds

After leaving the Spey estuary and gaining the shelter of the Moray Firth, these small silvery fish, some 15cm or less in length, now embark on a remarkably challenging journey of hundreds or thousands of kilometres to reach their traditional feeding grounds. These waters, teeming with edible marine life, are known at least to lie to the north of the Faeroe Islands and to the west and south of Greenland if not also further afield. Detailed information on the salmon's way of life at sea has for long been elusive. The stimulus that induces marine migration is unknown, as are its oceanic routes and possible navigational aids. The journey to the north has been reliably estimated to take four or five months. Thereafter several of the following months on the feeding grounds must inevitably be spent in sunless darkness, except when the scintillating Arctic winter sky may be illuminated by moonlight or by fleeting Aurora Borealis. However, salmon at different stages of their life are more active during darkness: downstream smolt migration takes place predominantly in the dark, as does the upstream movement of mature salmon in fresh water.

After their long journey they reap the benefit of voracious feeding on plankton and plankton dependent species as well as on a wide range of crustaceans and other marine life. They acquire the pink colour of mature salmon flesh attributable to the crustacean pigment astaxanthin. Weight gain is rapid and is ultimately dependent on the duration to which fish remain on the feeding grounds before returning to their birthplace to reproduce. Fish returning to fresh water after spending one winter at sea may weigh 1.5–3kg and are known as grilse. More commonly, fish spend two winters at sea and on return may weigh 6–10kg. Much larger fish may have remained feeding at sea for three or more years.

At sea the weight gain of fish that survive is remarkable but over the whole duration of the migration there is a large mortality rate. The total number of smolts leaving Spey annually for the feeding grounds is estimated to be of the order of half a million, whereas the total number of adult salmon returning annually to Spey may be around thirty to fifty thousand. Such assumptions are speculative and highly variable. A rough estimate is that the smolt run may be numbered in hundreds of thousands and the adult run in tens of thousands. While the mortality of smolts during downstream transit in the river and in the estuary may be significant and very likely more significant than previously believed, there appears to be huge loss of life either during marine migration, on the feeding grounds or during the return journey. Overall, survival from the egg stage is thought to be around five percent. The causes of such high attrition are largely speculative although there are known contributory factors such as commercial salmon fishing in Faroese and Greenland waters, by illegal interceptive trawl fishing on presumed migratory routes and as a by-catch of pelagic fishing.

Early Summer

Meantime, in early summer in Strathavon, the cuckoo's call, crisp and clear, even from distant woods, alerts a frisson of pleasure. No other bird foretells the advent of summer with such eclat.

As the season lengthens however, the skylark alone captures the essence of idyllic summer days. Blissful it is to lie in the warm grass of a fallow field as a skylark ascends in song, ever higher, ever fainter and finally no more. But, remarkably, as one lark is lost from sight and sound, another may rise to prolong the ecstatic experience.

Homeward Bound

O f the smolts on the feeding grounds, the small number maturing as grilse varies from year to year: in some years it may be substantial and in others quite modest. The main grilse run occurs in early summer and these fish, having spent a relatively short time at sea, are small. Their appearance is characteristic in being distinctly streamlined with a small head and a narrow wrist (junction of body with tail). After the main run in June or July, a small number of grilse return in later months and, having been longer at sea, these may weigh up to 5kg or more. They are often wrongly assumed by anglers to be 2SW (two sea winter) salmon. However, the majority of smolts return as 2SW fish. The pattern of their return during the year is reproducible but with some variation from year to year. In Spey, small numbers appear in the first two or three months of the year while the main runs are expected in April and May followed by smaller but significant numbers in June to September, tailing off to the end of the year.

The stimulus that prompts salmon to undertake the long journey home is presumably related to reproductive maturity. The accuracy with which the homeward journey of thousands of kilometres through featureless seas reaches the ultimate destination of their actual birthplace is remarkable. The factor or factors that subtend this phenomenal homing instinct are largely unknown. Also, the navigational aids guiding them during their return are just as obscure as those on which they depended during the outward journey. For much of their return journey the sun will not rise above the horizon. In darkness or in moonlight, do they depend on celestial topography? Are they influenced by magnetic fields? Or does the memory of the outward journey persist, hard wired in their rudimentary cerebral cortex? On reaching Scottish waters, salmon, which appear to swim within a few metres of the surface rather than at greater depth, tend to hug the coastline. Fish destined for Spey and its tributaries come from the west, following the coastline through the turbulent Pentland Firth turning south along the northeast coast into the Moray Firth. The accuracy with which they find their parent river in preference to other rivers flowing into the Moray Firth is believed to be through sense of smell. Although some irregularities may occur in terms of fish straying into the wrong river, such mistakes are usually later rectified as is confirmed by experiments involving the tagging of juvenile fish.

In the Estuary

When salmon arrive in the estuary they congregate there, often in considerable numbers, for a variable length of time until conditions, influenced mainly by volume of flow and water temperature, are propitious to induce their first run into the river. While resident in the estuary they are at significant risk of additional mortality. Although an instinct for self-preservation may alert them to flee from the approach of large aquatic species, many succumb to the superior water craft of rapacious dolphins, sometimes seen playfully tossing salmon in the air before devouring them, as well as to the voracity of the uncontrolled population of predatory seals.

The First Run

A rising level of water in Spey, sensed from the fresh water plume reaching far out into the estuary, is the usual stimulus responsible for the first committed run of salmon into the river. The size of the run may vary from a small number of fish in the earliest months of the year to a large shoal of a hundred or more in April or May. The speed of travel varies greatly but the first run may be long, reaching thirty or forty miles (50-60km) upstream in a matter of days. The long initial run is typical of early spring salmon destined for the higher spawning grounds. During the run they rest for variable lengths of time in intervening pools, sometimes briefly and sometimes for days or longer. The dramatic first run brings fish into holding pools high in the river though still distant from their final spawning destination. These early spring salmon may spend eight or nine months or even longer in fresh water before spawning, so that, after the first run, they may move from one holding pool to another at a considerably reduced pace.

We may imagine that in early March a female (hen) salmon, born six years earlier in the Loin Burn, came into the Spey estuary in the company of a small number of similar fish destined for the most distant spawning sites in A'en or high Spey tributaries. We may think of her as a beautiful fish weighing some 6kg, with gleaming silver flanks, tinged in incident light with a purple sheen. Behind a neat head her body swelled with potential power, replete with latent energy and primed for the challenge of the long run home.

Her gorging days over, her body fat stores were full. This sole caloric source would have to provide all her energy requirements during eight to nine months or longer until and after spawning. Remarkable though it may be to those unfamiliar with the fact, salmon do not feed at all in fresh water.

She waited with the other new arrivals in the estuary, venturing tentatively into and out of the river on tidal flows, poised to launch into her first long run dependent on the stimulus of a favourable change in water conditions. Once the winter had released its hold, the river, recently at a low level with floating clumps of ice and grue, was now running clear. Grue is a condition that occurs when ice forming on the riverbed rises to the surface, creating a liquid consistency of porridge. Warmer weather with melting snow in the distant hills saw the river level rise significantly and the water temperature rise by a few degrees above freezing point.

The small company of fish in the estuary would have been enlivened and energised by these changes. Their time had come; they were resolute and poised for action. When the late afternoon light began to fade and the clouds were tinged with orange, they continued to wait. But after the light had gone and darkness fell, they were off, the hen fish with them, forging like storm troopers against the flow of Spey. At times they seemed to rejoice in coming to the surface and slicing through it in an onward propulsive leap, characteristic of a running fish, in contrast to the dissimilar floppy leap of a resident fish. They made good progress through the lower pools and first paused to rest briefly in a holding pool upstream of Fochabers. Before daylight they were off again, through several pools of Gordon Castle and into the Orton water. Daylight was breaking as they broke the surface, rising head and tail in the glassy glide of the tail of Cairnty and took up temporary residence in that long and famous pool. When they entered the pool they encountered a resident population of kelts. Kelts are spent fish returning downstream in poor condition after having spawned the previous autumn. They are motivated to reach the sea and revisit the marine feeding grounds even to return to spawn for a second time. Unfortunately, few survive and successful second spawning is exceptional. Fresh fish appear to be attracted by other members of their species and are more inclined to tarry in a pool populated by kelts than in one that is vacant. The hen fish settled in the deepest part of the pool, resting against the rock face close to the right bank. An occasional flick of her tail fin was sufficient to maintain her sheltered resting station.

Fishing Begins

Whether day broke the pool was quiet but for the occasional splashy flop of a kelt. At the neck of the pool a dipper perched, pertly bobbing and intermittently diving, using its wings as oars in its submerged insect gathering. The light blanket of mist shrouding the distant hilltops would curl away in the warmth of what promised to be fine spring day. A light downstream wind gently ruffled the surface of the water.

The morning was well advanced when two anglers emerged from the fishing hut a short distance upstream and walked together down the grassy left bank towards the neck of Cairnty, disturbing a pair of sandpipers that rose and glided downstream on bowed wings, piping their waterside notes of spring.

The angler allocated Upper Cairnty hoped that mild weather and a rise in water level might have induced fish to run during the night. By day such running fish would be inclined to shelter in the deep water bathing the rock ledges which defined the far bank. He had tied on a popular hair-wing, yellow and black tube fly called a Tosh and began by wading across the shallower water at the neck of the pool sufficiently far that he would be able to drop a fly close to the far bank. He flexed the fifteen-foot (4.6m) rod in a series of short but lengthening casts until he was satisfied with the final length of line with which he aimed to cover the promising lies close to the rock ledges. He began fishing with aroused expectation.

Unlike trout fishing in which flies are designed to accurately imitate insect life forms, a salmon "fly" is a decided misnomer. There is no salmon fly that mimics any winged insect. Some are made to look like shrimps or prawns but the vast majority bears no resemblance to any aquatic creature, except that they may be vaguely fish-like. Salmon flies have evolved from what seems through experience and tradition to attract fish though the popularity of many is more dependent on what attracts fishermen.

The second angler began fishing from the left bank lower down the pool. His sensitivity was pleasurably evoked by the profusion of gorse (*Ulex europaeus*) on the left bank of lower Cairnty and already fully in bloom. Its rich yellow, sunlit blossom and warm sweet coconut scent brought him a sense of springtime rejuvenation. He was not at all discouraged by having drawn the lower part of Cairnty, knowing that there were "hot spots" where spring fish might lie right down to the promising glassy tail of the pool.

The first rod was now progressively covering the water at the neck, casting with a series of long and elegant Spey casts. He was clearly a master of this beautiful technique, sometimes described as poetry in motion. He consistently dropped the fly just short of the rock face but the strong current tended to draw it across the deep lies rather faster and with less depth than he would have preferred. The resting hen fish became aware of an object of interest, mobile in the current and seemingly animate, crossing her line of vision at a distance upstream. It repeatedly passed out of view to reappear ever nearer until it finally swam within easy reach and she was moved to intercept it. No one can answer the question, why? However, fresh fish new from the sea may retain for a time a latent feeding instinct that induces them to "take" an object reminiscent of any of the variety of marine species on which they were relatively recently gorging. In support of that theory, with passage of time in fresh water, fish are progressively less and less inclined to take an artificial fly.

A Fish Is Hooked

As the fly came towards the fish, she flicked her tail and rose from her lie. She lunged to intercept it but its approach in the current was fast and fleeting. With more ideal and deliberate presentation, the intercepted hook will commonly lodge in the scissors, the V-shaped intersection of upper and lower jaws, resulting in a secure hook-hold. In this case, although she succeeded in grasping the fly, the hook impinged superficially in harder tissue at the front of the lower jaw where the hold was likely to be less secure. In response to the resulting pull of water pressure on the line, the alerted angler raised his rod and applied strain. The fish immediately felt the foreign force pulling her head to the side and threatening to dislodge her from her lie. With brisk action of her tail fin she resisted and tried to maintain position but was drawn into the main current at the neck of the pool, and forced against her will to be pulled further across the pool towards the angler. With maximal effort she surged upstream against the strain as well as the strong current, gaining several yards of line before her strength was overcome. She turned downstream swimming fast and far. The reel sang with a high-pitched note, the exciting music of a hooked fish taking line. The angler stood his ground and in time gained control, drawing the salmon steadily upstream until once more level with his position. She was now beginning to tire and he was able to force her slowly across the pool towards his bank. Once unwillingly coerced into shallower water the salmon broke the surface to see the looming apparition of two men, the angler, with rod bent and the ghillie, poised on the bank with net at hand.

Provoked by this presumably hostile vision she summoned all her residual strength in a desperate final bid for freedom, wrenching her head to the side and thrashing her tail on the surface. Abruptly, she was rid of the mysterious force that had held her so firmly: the hook had lost its tenuous hold. Realisation of freedom took some seconds to sink in before she turned away, swimming unhindered to the safety of the deep.

The fisherman reeled in philosophically, checked his fly for any defect and waded out towards the bank. He sat with the ghillie for a few minutes contemplating the perceptible greening of new foliage on the distant trees that heralded the dawning of another year and the beginning of yet another fishing season. Nearby, on the pale coloured sandy shingle by the water's edge, two pied wagtails flitted from stone to stone, the male from time to time posturing in front of his future mate. A more colourful yellow-breasted grey wagtail bobbed and curtseyed at a distance.

The hen fish, recovering from exhausting exertion, returned to her original lie where she conserved energy, holding position with minimal effort. She would remain there at rest until moved to resume her upstream progress. Whether the recent experience registered in her consciousness as life-threatening is unknown but the fact that it resulted from snatching a salmon fly would certainly not deter her from doing so again in future weeks, days, hours or exceptionally even in minutes. In addition, sympathy with the salmon's plight may be a natural compassionate sentiment, although it is unknown whether the salmon's appreciation of suffering from stress, anxiety and panic is similar in intensity to what would be torment to the primate brain of mankind.

Onwards Upstream

In the afternoon, the wind veered to the north; the temperature fell and flurries of snow swept across the leaden water. The fishermen took shelter in the welcoming warmth of the hut. The next morning the river was a few centimetres lower. A covering of snow lay transiently on the bank. The air temperature was close to freezing point and the water temperature a few degrees higher. Snow whipping on the wind made fishing a dubious pleasure. The salmon, with body temperature reduced, lay torpid in deep water. As expected, the spring storm was transient and in a few days more seasonal warmth returned. The river began to rise from melting snow on distant high ground and the water temperature rose by a few degrees. These changes motivated the small pod of fish in Upper Cairnty to resume migratory activity. In the evening they became alert and poised to depart in darkness. In the gathering dusk, the silent flight of a woodcock or the twinkling of the first visible star in the darkening sky are said, according to fishing lore, to be when salmon are most likely to take a fly, a belief justified by the heightened state of animation that characterises fish about to continue their upstream journey.

Once darkness fell the salmon left the more placid deep water to move onwards into the forceful main stream, swimming hard and fast through intervening rough water and the remaining higher pools of Orton. They swam onwards through the famous beat of Delfur, resting briefly, and into Arndilly where at day-break they surfaced head and tail, one after another in the tail of the handsome holding pool named Cobble Pot. They would have paused there during daylight hours or for longer but for the disturbing appearance of an otter, its head only visible at first in the glide then surfacing intermittently for air as it searched higher into the body of the pool.

Salmon with room to manoeuvre in a large river are likely to comfortably out-swim an otter and if the otter should occasionally succeed in overpowering a salmon it would have to depend on stealth. In a small river in which a pursued salmon would be much more confined in terms of escape, an otter has a much greater chance of success. It is generally believed that the appearance of an otter in a pool ruins fishing prospects. If so it would imply that salmon are fully alert to the danger inherent in the approaching otter's sinuous form.

On leaving Cobble Pot, fish must ascend a stretch of rough water before reaching a small attractive pool in which they may rest. The character of pools such as these, in which confined flow is located above strong turbulent water, almost guarantees that every running salmon will pause there however briefly. Throughout the length of Spey there are few sites in which the above requirements are met such as they are in the renowned Jock's Tail. Arndilly anglers covet the opportunity of fishing Jock's Tail, in which there may so often be a chance of encountering one or more fish at rest and motivated to intercept an invitingly presented fly.

Here and there, depending on the time of year, small areas of the river bank are lit by a haze of blue, the purest blue of speedwell (*Veronica chamaedrys*) spreading its flowering tendrils through the moss. Amongst the many fishermen who tread by on their way to the river, some may be perceptive of the modest beauty of this tiny wild flower and the charm it brings to the waterside in spring and summer.

The fish continued on their upstream journey through the famous beats of middle Spey. They ran mainly during the hours of darkness, tending to rest in holding pools in daylight, often quite briefly, depending on favourable conditions for onward progress after nightfall. Low water or falling water temperature might induce them to stay for days, or even weeks, in any of the many large attractive pools in the river. In late spring and early summer these pools will be fished more than once during the day by one or more anglers and, should the pool hold travelling fish at rest, the chance of success will be high, especially if the angler returns to the pool in the evening.

A Fish Caught

The hen fish destined for the Loin Burn had safely negotiated miles of water where stretches of fast flowing turbulence were relieved by intermittent glides and deep sedate pools. She entered one of the most attractive pools on Spey, breaking the surface in a characteristic head and tail rise in the terminal glide. The pool was Polarder on Lower Pitchroy of the Knockando water. Had a fisherman seen the head and tail rise where the pool spilled over, he would have had high hopes of catching that fish in the body of the pool.

In the stillness of the evening when the air temperature was higher than the water, a solitary fisherman approached above the neck of the pool. He was using a floating line and had attached a Yellow Stoat's Tail, a small tube fly conceived and popularised at Park on the Aberdeenshire Dee. The tiny fly was fished round subsurface from deep to shallow water, progressively covering the possible lies in the pool. The hen fish saw the small lively object approaching ever nearer until it was comfortably within reach. Once again we do not know why she decided to intercept it but she rose from her lie and leisurely took it into her mouth before turning back again. The leisurely take was ideal and the hook lodged in the scissors. In response to the take the fisherman exerted firm strain and prepared to play the fish. The sequence of events mirrored the tussle described in Upper Cairnty except that in warmer water with seasonal lighter tackle the fish tended to be livelier. It was finally subdued and led towards the shingle where it could be carefully pushed from the shallow water to expose its head. The fisherman quickly dislodged the hook and turned the fish to face the direction of flow where the current was sufficient to carry oxygenated water through its gills. Within minutes, recovering from exhaustion, it tentatively flicked its tail. A more purposeful flick was sufficient to release it from the fisherman's hands and back towards deeper water. Returning the salmon, apparently unharmed, was in accord with the now widely adopted policy of conservation, "catch and release". This fish had been carefully handled and would soon recover to resume its onward progress, albeit at risk of being caught again, even more than once. The morality of subjecting a fish to the stress of capture and then release with the ever present risk of repetition in contrast to killing it smartly as a food source, is a vexed issue.

Leaving Spey

With recovering sweeps of her tail fin she regained the deep water of the pool to rest for some days before resuming upstream progress towards the well-known Junction Pool on Ballindalloch where A'en tumbled into Spey. In the Junction Pool there were several other resident fish, a few of which were genetically A'en fish though most were destined to spawn in the headwaters of Spey and its smaller tributaries.

In early June, when A'en was low and fish disinclined to enter it, a thunder storm in distant Badenoch saw a dramatic rise of water in Spey, which induced an immediate exodus of salmon from the Junction Pool. Several A'en fish were temporarily waylaid into joining this upstream surge, straying as far as the secluded lower reaches of the Tulchan water. The diverted fish settled temporarily in the long Wood Pool, within sight of the former Honeymoon Hut, which for so many years graced the lower beat of Tulchan.

The hut was said to have been a gift from the renowned fisherman George McCorquodale, fondly known as *The Great Salmon Slayer of the Spey,* to his daughter on her marriage. The outlook of the original Honeymoon Hut, as it stood for generations, was enhanced by several clumps of wild lupins (*Lupinus perennis*), flowering on the grassy bank leading down to the river, their colourful spires rising in hues of blue. But the charm of the adjacent secluded flowering of the exquisitely beautiful heart's ease *(Viola tricolour)* was savoured only by those who knew where to find it.

Within days, as the water dropped, the salmon that had strayed beyond their true destination gradually fell back downstream to regain the Junction Pool. The correction of their temporary dislocation was presumably attributable to their remarkably olfactory sensitivity in detecting the characteristic difference in the water odour of A'en in contrast to that of Spey. Restored to the quiet depths of the Junction Pool, these fish waited as before for favourable conditions for onward progress. A modest increase in water level was sufficient to induce the A'en fish to surge through its turbulent confluence with Spey and upstream into the Ballindalloch water. After some miles of progress, pausing temporarily in pools and deep glides, the mouth of Livet was in sight and the salmon destined for Livet and its small tributaries in the Braes of Glenlivet left the main group.

Within a short walk of the junction of Livet with A'en, after the early days of summer have brought warmth and longer light, a plant of distinction might, by dint of privileged local knowledge or simply good fortune, be found in bloom in a small area, less than a metre square. The flower, *Linnea borealis*, named after the Swedish botanist Carl Linnaeus whose favourite plant it is said to have been, is a small elusive woodland gem, quite common in Scandinavia but relatively rare in Scotland. Nevertheless, it may be found in small colonies, as in this case, at the margin of conifer woodland where the captivating sight of its delicate pink nodding bell-flowers is likely to be memorable.

Onward Into A'enside

The main run, modest in number, continued upstream into the secluded glen of A'enside where flights of curlews, rising from their nesting sites on the lower slopes of the Cromdales, often make a memorable impression. They float in the air, gliding on extended wings, sounding their melancholy bubbling call that travels far through the glen in a distant and poignant evocation of wilderness.

In the fading light of a summer evening the stillness may sometimes be enlivened by a weird humming sound: the drumming of a snipe. This distinctive music of the snipe's courtship display is produced by vibration of specific tail feathers during demonstrative diving flight. To hear it in the gathering dusk of a fugitive day evokes a comforting sense of being at one with nature in the solitude of remote moors.

In early summer, during their continued upward journey through A'enside, the fish would pass in sight of several smallholdings, some no longer inhabited, that stand on higher ground above the river. At the gable end of one of these habitations there grew an aged gnarled rose bush. It flowered sparsely but its white flowers, though small, were intensely perfumed. I imagine this to be the variety that Hugh MacDiarmid immortalised, with so moving emotion in so few words, in his poem *The Little White Rose.*

The small pod of salmon continued their upstream journey, some resting temporarily in the Milton Stream, a deep run rather than a pool. In the Milton Stream, as well as in similar lies in which, with experience, resting salmon may be detected from a high vantage point, they were in the past at risk of being surreptitiously foul hooked (hooked involuntarily anywhere in the body). Amongst a previous generation of A'enside fishers there were a few highly skilled local exponents of this art, which produced a fresh fish to enliven the humdrum table as well as the tables of grateful neighbours. The practice was of course frankly illegal and legitimate fishermen will have welcomed its demise.

The Milton Burn

The Milton Burn, which joins A'en along with the River Lochy above the Milton Stream, rises on the high plateau linking West and East Cromdale and descends between their steep shoulders, beneath the landmark blue rocks to the east. Its subsequent course through lower ground towards its termination includes an area of peat bog, distinguished by a large expanse of bog myrtle (*Myrica gale*), a plant rightly celebrated for its aromatic resinous scent. Whenever one may come across this remarkable plant, the opportunity of crushing a sprig of leaves to release the unique perfume is an experience to be cherished. For those who knew it in their youth, the distinctive scent of bog myrtle in later years will surely flood their senses with distant memories of the halcyon days of a highland childhood.

In areas of the peat bog, mounds of sphagnum moss form a colourful under-carpet in shades of green, red, pink and orange, lighting up the dark green uniformity of bog myrtle foliage. And the landscape of the damp ground beyond the bog myrtle is lit by the colourful sulphur yellow spires of bog asphodel (*Narthecium ossifragum*).

In the damp ground another plant, fascinating for its insectivorous aptitude, may be in bloom. The flowers of common butterwort (*Pinguicula vulgaris*), also known as bog violet or marsh violet, are solitary nodding funnel-shaped trumpets of deep blue or purple, held high on upright stalks. Butterworts are sparsely distributed and, while the blooms are beautiful, the plant's reputation draws particular attention to the star-shaped basal leafy rosette. The surface of the yellowish-green fleshy leaves, lying flat on the ground, is coated with a sticky secretion attractive to insects. On entrapment of an insect on the sticky surface the leaf edges slowly roll in to close over it in the beginning of a digestive process that augments the limited nutritional resources of the peat bog.

High above the Milton Burn on the north-eastern shoulder of West Cromdale there is a large expanse of cloudberry (*Rubus chamaemorus*). For most of the year its large-leafed foliage flourishes in a distinctive carpet above the undergrowth of lichen but in early August the modest climb to reach their location may be rewarded by a bounty of delicious, large uniquely-flavoured yellow berries so esteemed as a delicacy in Scandinavia. Unfortunately, in Scotland, lacking reliable snow cover, cloudberries in flower are susceptible to spring frosts and subsequent fruiting from one year to the next is erratic. However, should the long climb be unproductive in terms of quantity of berries, it may be rewarded by hearing the plaintive piping of a golden plover. There is no other birdcall of the remote high ground so forlorn and so evocative of the spiritual essence of mountain wilderness.

The Upper Reaches of A'en

By mid August the salmon were near Tomintoul. The heather (*Calluna vulgaris*) was now in full bloom and the slopes of the surrounding hills were clothed in their annual richly-coloured deep pink carpet. Now is the best time to tread through the springing heather with every step releasing clouds of pollen and the scent of heather honey hanging in the air. During August in Glenavon, the hills become alive, not with music but with a daily fusillade of gunshot. Commencing traditionally on the 12th of August and continuing on most weekdays into September, the grouse shooting season brings life and colour into the glen.

Roads by the banks of A'en, usually quiet and empty, become noisy thoroughfares for vehicles transporting guests and beaters from one location to another. Welcome employment is available for the young and fit as grouse-beaters as well as for the more mature as loaders. In addition, the idiosyncrasies of the well-heeled imported guests, fondly and amusingly known as the "toffs", are a frequent source of ridicule and fun.

Some of the salmon took up temporary residence in the Delvorar Pool, a short distance upstream of the entrance to the Inchrory Estate. The pool, though not particularly large, is deep and is crossed by a road-bridge. Those who cross the bridge in autumn and know what may be seen from this vantage point, seldom miss the chance of gazing into the underlying depths, to marvel at the serried ranks of waiting salmon destined for higher spawning grounds.

The Loin hen fish continued to move upstream, pausing temporarily in small pools on the Inchrory water until early October when she reached her last resting destination of the Loin Pool. She would remain there along with other male and female salmon until her final spawning run into the Loin Burn in November. This fish had been in fresh water for many months without food and was therefore much thinner and weaker than when she came into Spey from the sea. In addition, her appearance had gradually changed from sparkling silver to a tarnished dull grey colour. Male fish in the Loin Pool had changed more dramatically. At the beginning of their fresh water run they were also objects of beauty in pristine silver but by October they were markedly discoloured in mottled shades of red and orange.

In addition the males had grown a "kype". When fresh from the sea both cock and hen fish show a small projection, no more than a few millimetres long, at the front extremity of the lower jaw, slightly more prominent in the male. As the time of spawning approaches this projection increases dramatically in size in males, especially in large fish, even to the extent of bulging into and sometimes penetrating the soft tissue of the upper jaw.

It is termed a kype and may have evolved as a spear-like projection to fend off rivals during mating. Late autumn fish, both male and female, are referred to as "coloured" even though females lack much of an element of colour. They are in poor condition with grossly diminished fat stores and are of little value as a food source.

By the time the hen salmon had settled into the Loin Pool, nightly frost had crisped the withered grasses on the river banks. The birches in the lower glen were clothed in mantles of yellow ochre and swathes of bracken in rich tones of burnt sienna. The slopes of Ben A'en, recently resplendent in heather bloom, were now suffused in sombre shades of grey and brown, contributing to the melancholy evocation of autumn that pervaded the landscape of upper Speyside.

The Red Deer Rut

About mid October, with some variation from year to year, the red deer rut begins. Groups of stags that had spent most of the year together in harmony begin to disperse as the larger individuals seek to gather hinds coming into season into a personal harem. Mature stags wander widely in search of hinds, sometimes picking up small unattached groups and challenging for supremacy over larger groups commandeered by another stag.

Stags intent upon mating often roll in wet peat hags, giving their coat, especially the long hair of the neck and mane, a dark and threatening appearance of exaggerated size. The most dramatic feature of the rut however, is the roaring of impassioned stags. The roar, which is a deep-throated, heart-rending bellow, is an expression of challenge, as in confronting a rival stag with the intention of seizing possession of his hinds or that of defiance in defence of prior ownership. Confrontation may result in a physical battle in which antlers are locked in a struggle for supremacy in which weight is the determinant factor. There is no more magical music to the ears of deer-stalkers and their ilk than the distant roar of a wandering stag and no sound so redolent of the remote highlands in the shortening days of late autumn.

In October, the high corries resonate with the roaring of impassioned stags and the deer-stalking season brings seasonal drama to Glenavon. By spying the high ground early in the day, a traditional deer-pony might be located at a distant vantage point waiting for the signal that a carcass is ready to be uplifted. And the stalking party of two or three individuals on the distant slopes of Ben A'en might also be visible in their approach to the stalk of a selected stag. It would seldom be possible, however, for an observer, spying from a considerable distance, to follow their final movements as they take cover behind every available irregularity in terrain. Once the chosen firing point has been gained and the rifle slid forward in readiness, inconvenient intrusion of intervening hinds or quite often the need to wait for a specific stag to rise from recumbency to present a broadside target, could sometimes mean considerable delays of inactivity. Apart from infrequent whispered observations between stalker and rifle, long interludes of patient waiting and watching are passed in reflective silence, broken only by the soft rustle of windblown grasses or occasionally by the distant plaintive bleating of a golden plover. But when the time to shoot is propitious, the boom of the high velocity rifle reverberating round the rock-girt crags of the mountainous amphitheatre sounds a dramatic conclusion to a completed stalk.

The deer pony may soon be seen moving towards a convenient point where the stag will be loaded. As the loaded pony makes its slow but steadfast way downward towards the track leading ultimately to the larder, the day is far advanced. But diminishing daylight does not compromise the sharp vision of three ravens appearing on high, gliding and flapping on purposeful descent. Their characteristic raucous croaking may celebrate the discovery of fresh entrails with the promise of an evening's gorging. They make a sinister impression and a discordant sound to the stalking party on its way downhill and onwards towards home. In fading light the temperature falls and gusting wind from the north bears flurries of swirling snowflakes that sting their cheeks in a forewarning of forthcoming winter harshness on the high ground.

The Final Journey Home

By the end of October, with the stalking season over, the glen fell silent for a brief period before the estate stalkers began the arduous hind cull, which would occupy them daily, often in bitter weather, for many weeks.

On a sombre November night the hen salmon left the Loin Pool in a purposeful upstream surge that brought to a conclusion her long journey home. As she instinctively searched the lower reaches of the Loin Burn for a rough gravel bed of adequate size, she was shadowed by a sizeable cock fish in florid autumn colours. The large and ugly kype, protruding grotesquely from his lower jaw, added to his menacing appearance and was waged aggressively in intimidating rival males. Except for such pugnacious diversions in protection of his exclusive mating rights, the cock fish seldom left the side of his broody companion.

A suitable bed of gravel selected, the female salmon began its excavation. Lying on her side she repeatedly flapped her tail fin in a vigorous action that displaced gravel laterally and inferiorly. In time a trench some 15-20cm both deep and wide and some 50-75cm long was created while her intended mate maintained his close attentive station. As the hen began the spawning process, releasing several thousand eggs in a continuous stream into the trench, the male participated in a climactic emotional experience characterised by prominent quivering. It coincided with the male's release of a cloud of thin milky fluid (milt) effectively coating and thereby fertilising the mass of eggs. Although the cock fish may have successfully chased away rival adult salmon, the several sexually mature precocious parr that sneakily tried to contribute their milt tended to be ignored. Once the eggs had been bathed in milt and the mating ceremony was over, the hen fish began the completion of her life's work by covering the spawn with several centimetres of the previously excavated gravel. The remarkable life cycle of the salmon was now ready to be repeated by a new generation.

The Fate of Kelts

Salmon after spawning are in poor physical condition. They are termed kelts and many are painfully thin, with body fat stores exhausted, their flesh soft and flabby, their bellies sagging, their vents gaping open and their strength hugely diminished. Some succumb to an early death though several drift quietly back into A'en, making their way downstream on the flow, or are swept onwards by the force of winter floods. Kelts are susceptible to fungal disease and many die in transit though a significant number do survive to reach Spey, where they congregate in lower Spey pools by the following spring. Although many of these will show the characteristic features of physical decline, some of them do begin to regain condition in fresh water. Presumably they may recover their feeding instinct as evidenced by their voracity towards artificial lures. This apparent recovery, with restoration of a bright silvery appearance, and the readiness with which they are caught at the beginning of the new season, commonly fools inexperienced anglers to mistake what is termed a well-mended kelt for a fresh fish.

Presumably downstream migration of spawned fish is influenced by inherent motivation to return to the sea. Despite their emaciated state it is remarkable that a small minority of kelts do succeed in negotiating the long and hazardous journey to reach the oceanic feeding grounds for a second time. And, given good fortune, they may even return to spawn once again. However, the large majority do not survive and, in the following spring, the occasional sight of their carcasses, disfigured by disease or ravaged by predators, lying rotting on riverbanks makes a poignant ending to a remarkable life.

About the Author

Norman Matheson, a retired surgeon, was captivated by nature from his boyhood in upper Speyside. As a lifelong salmon fisherman he is known throughout the Spey and Aberdeenshire Dee. He has published extensively and has illustrated children's picture books. He was awarded an MBE for voluntary work in the visual arts.